CHANGE

MEETING GOD IN CHANGE

Stephen D. Eyre

6 studies for individuals or groups

GW00504086

Scripture Union

MEETING GOD BIBLE STUDIES

Scripture Union, 207-209 Queensway, Bletchley, MK2 2EB, England.

e-mail: info@scriptureunion.org.uk

Internet: http://www.scripture.org.uk/

©1999 by InterVarsity Christian Fellowship/USA

First published in the United States by InterVarsity Press
First published in Great Britain by Scripture Union, 2000

Cover photograph: Roberta Polfus

ISBN 1 85999 403 2

Printed in Great Britain by Ebenezer Baylis & Son, The Trinity Press, Worcester and London.

Contents

INTRODUCING
Meeting God in Change

Change happens to us all the time, in a variety of ways. Growing requires change as we move from infancy to adulthood. Learning requires change as we go from high school to college and from college to our career.

I know a few things about change and what it does to us. My family has moved six or seven times (depending on whether you count moving twice in the same city) in the last twenty-five years.

Change happens at different levels. On a superficial level, there is the change of fads and fashion. On another level, there are changes in our lifestyle brought about by technology. On an even deeper level, changes in socially defined roles in the marketplace and family shift and influence us in ways that we may feel yet only dimly perceive. Culture shock is a term that was coined to describe what happened when a person moved from one culture to another—say from the United States to Japan. It can also happen within our own culture.

For many reasons, like it or not, change happens. The good news is that God meets his people in the midst of all of life's changes. In fact, times of change afford a special opportunity to catch a glimpse of God in ways that we may never have seen before, and to grow in intimacy with him.

The Shape of This Guide
Intimacy with God is what God had in mind when he called Abram (who later became Abraham) to change. Study one is about Abram's call. Leaving all that was familiar, Abram packed up his

belongings and followed God to a promised land.

Being called away to an intimate knowledge of God is a pretty unnerving business. The Israelites discovered that the inward enemies of fear and unbelief can stand in the way of the liberating changes that God intends to produce. In the Israelites' Red Sea experience, we will find liberating dimensions of confession and courage.

Godly change is not merely for the sake of change. It means that we are called on a journey from one place to another. Studying a portion of 1 Corinthians 12, we will discover that God has a new place and a new role for us to fill in the body of Christ.

Silence, listening and reflecting are skills that we need to hear God as he calls us out and directs us on our journey. So we will spend time meditating on Psalm 32 in study four.

Changing is hard work and requires energy. Just as we are not to live on bread alone, so we must learn to renew our strength on the spiritual food that God's Spirit feeds us. Through the words of the prophet Isaiah, we will enjoy a banquet at God's invitation.

Finally, changing requires battling against heavy opposition that can unsettle us and wear us down. Returning to Abram's story in study six, we will learn that it is permissible to ask in faith for the assurance of God's promises in the midst of turbulence and conflict.

God is with us. Wherever we are in our experiences of challenge, change and transition, he is working for his glory and our good. This guide provides a few tools to help us discern God's presence in the midst of change. Seeing him at work in the changing circumstances of life, we will find strength to cope with the difficulties that we face and the courage to do what needs to be done.

Practising the Disciplines

Each of the studies focuses on a different spiritual discipline that takes us deeper into the topic.

1. *Scripture study:* we begin with an inductive study that reveals what the Bible has to say about the topic.

2. *Confession:* we look at ourselves in the light of Scripture, taking time in the midst of Bible study for silent reflection and repentance.

3. *Community:* we move to interaction with others around a passage or an exercise, asking for guidance and encouragement as we seek God.

4. *Silence:* again we come before Scripture, but this time seeking not to analyze but to hear God's voice and guidance for us.

5. *Obedience:* in the light of Scripture's teaching we make commitments to change.

6. *Prayer:* we take time to seek God, weaving prayer through our encounter with Scripture.

These sessions are designed to be completed in 45 minutes to an hour in a group, or 30 minutes in personal study. However, feel free to follow the leading of the Holy Spirit and spend as long as is needed on each study.

Every session has several components.

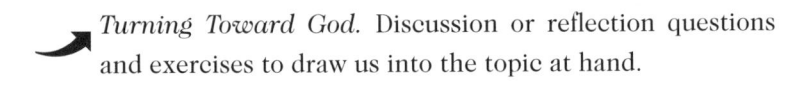

Turning Toward God. Discussion or reflection questions and exercises to draw us into the topic at hand.

Receiving God's Word. A Bible study with application and spiritual exercises.

Now or Later. Ideas that can be used at the end of the study during a time of quiet for a group or an individual.

Alternatively, these ideas can be used between studies during quiet times.

The components of this guide can help us to meet God with both our minds and hearts. May they encourage you through times of change.

1

CALLED TO CHANGE

·····························

Practising the Discipline of Scripture Study

"Take a risk and come join me in England." I didn't hear a voice, but I heard those words. Were they an invitation from God or an expression of my own wanderlust?

For a month or more my wife Jackie and I had been seeking the Lord's will for our next step. We had been invited by the director of an overseas mission to fill a vacant post in London, working among American students in study-abroad programs. We were interested, but we weren't sure it was the right move. Our three boys were twelve and under, and an overseas move would require big adjustments of all of us.

During this time I had a speaking engagement in Knoxville. While driving back to our home in Nashville, I had been prayerfully mulling over our choices. When I was ready for a break to shake my road-induced grogginess, I saw a bowling alley and thought that a quick game would clear my head. It was as I put my hand on the door to walk in that I heard those words and felt a sense of call.

Despite our initial uncertainty, the next months and years confirmed it.

We were called to ministry, but calling is not merely for those in ministry. God has a purpose for all of us as we follow him in every situation we find ourselves: mothers, fathers, executives, teachers and plumbers. Abram may have felt the same uncertainty when he received a call to begin a journey that would bring change for him, his family and, over the centuries, millions and millions of others. Like Abram, the father of the faith, sometimes in our lives we all wonder what God is calling us to and what changes it will require.

TURNING TOWARD GOD   ✲What attachments do you have to the place and the relationships (family, friends) in which you grew up?

✲ If you have moved away from that place you first knew as home, what was difficult about it?

How did those changes affect your relationship to God?

✲ If you have lived in the same area all of your life, what do you think might be the most difficult for you to part with?

✲It has been suggested that the call to faith is a call to leave whether we stay in the same place or not. How might it be possible to leave in order to follow the call of God and yet not physically move?

The Discipline of Scripture Study

God's Word is one of our greatest resources for knowing him and drawing close to him. What follows is an inductive Bible study that will help you draw out the truths of Scripture for yourself through three types of questions: observation (to gather the facts), interpretation (to discern the meaning) and application (to relate the truths of Scripture to our lives).

 RECEIVING GOD'S WORD   1. Read Genesis 12:1-9. God gives Abram a challenging call and an attractive set of inducements and assurances. In your own words, what are God's promises to Abram (vv. 1-3, 7)?

2. What anxieties and difficulties might Abram have experienced as he considered this radical change in his life?

3. Considering that only Ishmael and Isaac were born to Abram, what can we learn about the way God keeps his promises?

4. If Abram responds to God's call to an unknown future, God is going to give him the desires of his heart. What are the desires of your heart?

How might the call of God shape your heart's desires?

5. Look at verses 4-5. Abram didn't set off on this adventure of faith by himself. Describe the group that made the journey.

6. In your experience what are the benefits and tensions of going through times of change with those you care for?

7. When we are called to move on, we need assurances that we are going where we are supposed to. How has God assured you that you are in the "right" place? (Or, if you are still on the way, what sort of confirmation are you anticipating?)

8. While moving around in the land, how does Abram show the importance of his relationship with God (vv. 7-8)?

9. We no longer build altars when we have a spiritual encounter. How can you call on the name of the Lord in your time of transition and change?

10. What insights and assurances can you take from these verses as you seek to meet with God in a time of transition and change?

11. When have you been tempted to turn away from the Lord's call on your life because the change it requires is difficult?

12. What insights can you glean from this passage in coping with God's call and the changes it requires?

God calls us to let go of our wordly means of security to follow him. Ask God to give you the courage to follow his call in the adventure of faith.

NOW OR LATER   Take time to reflect on how change and transition affect you. Write down your feelings, hesitations, concerns and anxieties. Also make a note of how change and transition affects your relationships with others. Consider, too, how it affects your times of worship and prayer with God. When you are done, sit for a while, asking God to give the quiet assurance of his presence now and for the coming months.

Compare Genesis 12:1 with Mark 1:16-18. Although separated by at least 2,000 years, God met both Abram and the disciples with a call to leave and follow. Consider the similarities and differences in these calls.

2

GIVING OUR
FEARS TO GOD

·····························

Practising the Discipline
of Confession

By the time we had been in England for three weeks, I was questioning God. The housing we expected fell through. If we didn't find something soon, we were going to be out on the street.

While the boys were occupied on the playground equipment, Jackie and I talked about our next steps. I recall staring at the ground through a haze of anxiety. My confusion was no doubt enhanced by culture shock and emotional fatigue generated by the unfamiliar. I wondered, *Did I really hear the Lord? Is God really with us? What kind of a father am I to drag my family into this?*

Our confessions during times of change and transition will not be the traditional "God, I've broken your laws and need to tell you that I have sinned." Instead, our confession will be more along the lines of a panicky accusation, "God, I don't trust you, and I think you have led me to a dead end of failure and destruction."

God is not put off by our fears but takes them on as he moves us to the new freedoms he intends for us. He knows that change brings anxiety and fear. Despite our fears, he wrestles us away from our familiar but confining past into the freedom of a faithful future.

 TURNING TOWARD GOD   *Sometimes we sense God's presence. Sometimes we sense his absence. Whether we sense him or not, he is still present. How do you relate to God when you sense his presence?

*How do you relate to God when you sense his absence?

The Discipline of Confession

God calls us to confess our sin and our fear to him and to one another. Confession is an opportunity to ask for God's help and mercy. Interacting with Scripture will help you open your heart to God. Along the way you will have some opportunities to confess your own sin. You may want to do this verbally, silently or in writing. Follow God's leading.

RECEIVING GOD'S WORD   1. Read Exodus 14:5-12. At the sight of the approaching Egyptian army, Moses is confronted with a series of fear-driven questions by the Israelites. What reasons would the Israelites have to be so afraid of Pharaoh?

2. Our present fears are frequently rooted in our painful experiences of the past. What previous painful experiences bring you anxiety in times of change?

Take time now to bring those fears to God in prayer.

3. Read Exodus 14:13-14. Fight and flight are the classic responses to fear. What is Moses' response to the Israelites panic?

4. Standing still in the face of danger requires both courage and confidence. What reasons did the Israelites have for believing Moses?

5. What reasons do you have for courage and confidence in the face of threatening uncertainty?

6. Read Exodus 14:15-18. While Moses told the Israelites to stand firm, God says move out. How is it possible to stand firm *and* move out in the same situation?

7. Look at verses 14-18 again. Describe God's purpose and perspective on the impending danger.

8. Every change and new opportunity has elements of risk and even danger. What do you think are God's purposes in your life now, and how will he gain glory through what you are going through?

9. Read Exodus 14:19-28. Pharaoh and his army are eradicated. Describe Moses' and God's roles in the battle.

10. Three times we read about Moses stretching out his hand over the sea (vv. 15, 21, 26). If all power belonged to God, why did Moses need to do anything at all?

11. Stretching out our hands is a physical posture of prayer. In what ways might God be asking you to "stretch out your hand" toward the challenges you face?

12. Read Exodus 14:29-31. After the Israelites experienced the saving power of God, they moved from fearful terror of Pharaoh and his army (v. 10) to fear and trust of the "Lord and Moses his servant." What is the difference between "fearful anxiety" of circumstances and "fearful trust" in the Lord?

13. Proverbs 1:7 says, "The fear of the LORD is the beginning of . . . wisdom." What is required for you to move from a foolish fear of circumstances to a wise fear of the Lord?

Sometimes trusting the Lord means standing still, sometimes it means moving forward. Ask God to give you the discernment to know what he is requiring of you at this point in your life.

NOW OR LATER   Confession can be silent, verbal (alone or with others) or written. Which of these methods comes most naturally to you? Push yourself outside your comfort zone by trying one or more of the other methods. As part of this, you may also want to experiment with your physical posture in prayer and confession. Pray with your hands outstretched or on your knees or perhaps lying prostrate on the floor.

3

FINDING MY NEW PLACE

....

Practising the Discipline
of Community

Singular is not a word we use anymore. We might hear it in a period movie or read it in a novel about life in England a century or so ago. It means "strange, odd, unusual and out of place." Some of us may want to stand out from the crowd and make our mark. (I'm one of them.) But few of us want to be "singular." During times of transition and change, however, we may indeed become singular. Whether we physically move or not, something happens that alters our routine social patterns and connections. We feel out of place and wonder whether we belong. That's why the church is such a great gift of the Lord.

The Discipline of Community
God gives us other people in the body of Christ for support and encouragement, as well as enjoyment. As we learn about Christ from Scripture and from each other, we are made complete. For the following exercises and Scripture study you need to work with one or two others or a small group. Ask someone you trust to work

through this material with you. (This could be a spouse, but it would be good to include a friend as well.)

 TURNING TOWARD GOD   ✳What support has the Christian community provided for you in times of transition and change?

✳During times of transitions and change, our social inclinations tend to become more extreme. Some withdraw, others intensify their social activity. What do you do?

✳How can (or does) God meet you in the midst of your need?

 **RECEIVING GOD'S WORD**   **1.** Read 1 Corinthians 12:12-13. Paul writes that all Christians share a common unity. What is it that unifies us?

2. How have you experienced that shared social unity in the church(es) you have been a part of?

3. Social status (slave or free) and race (Jew or Greek) are potential barriers to experiencing interconnectedness as Christians. In your experience how do these keep us disconnected?

4. Read 1 Corinthians 12:14-31. The body is the image that the apostle Paul uses to unfold the dynamics of Christian community. What part of the body would you use to characterize your place in the Christian community?

5. What do you enjoy about being a member of the body?

What do you struggle with?

6. Sometimes, especially during times of transition and change, we may have a new role to play or a different function in the body. What difficulties can arise when this happens?

7. The apostle Paul's prescription for dealing with barriers in the body of Christ begins with an affirmation of diversity (vv. 14-20). How can understanding diversity help you when you feel like you don't fit in?

8. Paul's prescription for dealing with barriers continues with an affirmation of mutual interdependence in verses 21-26. How can understanding interdependence help when you don't feel like fitting in?

9. Paul shifts from speaking about body parts to spiritual gifts (vv. 27-31). How do each of the gifts he mentions contribute to the healthy functioning of the body of Christ?

10. What potential problems come up when Christians begin to discuss the use of the gifts mentioned here?

11. Take a few moments to reflect on the spiritual gift(s) you think God has given you. Make a note of your reflections.

Now consider what gifts God has given your partner or others in your small group.

Discuss your ideas with each other.

12. How will using your gift(s) for others help you personally in times of change in your life?

God has gifted certain people to meet your needs for this time in your life. He has given you gifts to meet the needs of others and is placing you into changing situations that will open up new opportunities to use them. Ask him to make you open to give and to receive the gifts of the Spirit.

NOW OR LATER When things change we need to see how we fit in the new situation. For some of us, this is a delightful challenge of social exploration. For others, it is a difficult time that takes great effort and energy. No matter whether we move into new social connections easily or not, we need to know that we are connected with others and have a contribution to make. As we find our place, the new situation begins to feel like home.

Reflect on your sense of past connections. What did you enjoy about them? What did you find difficult?

What about your current sense of connections? How are they changing? How are the changes affecting you?

Consider one or two steps you can take this next week to develop and enhance a new set of connections.

4

DISCERNING GOD'S DIRECTION

·····································

Practising the Discipline of Silence

Ever lie in bed at night worrying about whether you made the right decision? This can happen any time—but we are especially susceptible to this during times of transition and change. We lie in bed rehearsing the situation over and over in a restless litany. Of course, that seldom gets us anywhere. In finding our way through the jungle of choices there comes a time when we need to stop and listen.

The Discipline of Silence

For many of us the disciplines of silence and meditation are the most difficult to pursue. We want to complete a task—read through a book of the Bible or pray through a list of needs. Sometimes, however, God wants us simply to come before him and wait to hear his voice. The Bible study below is best done in quiet, whether you are in a room with others in your small group or alone. After you have completed all the questions on your own, then you may discuss them with a group.

TURNING TOWARD GOD   ✻What worries you about decisions you have made in the past month?

✻How have you seen God involved in your life the past month?

✻Consider, are there ways that you may be blocking out God's guidance and care? To help you with this reflection, you might see yourself as a child who keeps talking so she won't hear her parents instructions. Or perhaps you inwardly have your fingers in your ears? Spend a few moments in quiet. Inwardly stop talking and filling your mind with words, and then take your fingers out of your ears. Relax, settle down and listen. After you have settled down inside, jot down a few notes on the state of your heart.

 **RECEIVING GOD'S WORD 1.** Read the following passage through several times.

⁶Therefore let everyone who is godly pray to you
    while you may be found;
surely when the might waters rise,
    they will not reach him.
⁷You are my hiding-place;
    you will protect me from trouble
    and surround me with songs of deliverance.

⁸I will instruct you and teach you in the way you should go;
    I will counsel you and watch over you.
⁹Do not be like the horse or the mule,

which have no understanding
but must be controlled by bit and bridle
or they will not come to you.
[10]Many are the woes of the wicked,
   but the LORD's unfailing love
   surrounds the man who trusts in him.

[11]Rejoice in the LORD and be glad, you righteous;
   sing, all you who are upright in heart! *(Psalm 32:6-11)*

2. Ask God to guide you to the verses that will speak to you.

3. Read the passage again slowly.

4. What words or phrases stand out to you?

5. How do these words address the needs in your life?

6. What message does God have for you today?

7. Spend five or ten minutes listing the things that worry you. Use a number of small sheets of paper to write down each item separately. Be honest, noting even those things that may seem foolish or frivolous. God cares about what bothers you.

Look carefully at your lists. Which are things that are out of your control? In *Meditative Prayer* Richard Foster suggests putting each of these worries into an imaginary box, but you might want to make it a real box. This box is your gift to God. Try to imagine giving this present to God. How does he respond?

For each of the other items write down one or two simple steps you could take to deal with them in the near future. Decide on one or two to work on in the upcoming weeks. How will the steps you take affect your ability to rest?

Allow the words from Scripture about God's care for us to fill your prayers with praise for the gift of rest in the midst of every circumstance.

 **NOW OR LATER**   "As we compose ourselves in mind and body for sleep, we should think of ourselves as releasing the mind and body into the loving arms of God."   ST. TERESA

Each night this week as you go to sleep, remind yourself that you are resting in God's care. By turning your sleep over to God you will be taking a first step toward giving him all of your concerns.

Before you go to bed and when you wake up, write in your journal about your experiences of becoming quiet and listening for his presence with a settled heart.

5

RESOURCES FOR THE JOURNEY

··

Practising the Discipline of Obedience

During times of growth and change we need lots of food, good food. Parents of teenagers hear the refrigerator door open and shut on a minute-by-minute basis. All of us need to grow and eat throughout our lives. What we forget, or perhaps never learned, is that physical food only goes so far. Our souls need good food and lots of it. It comes, however, not by opening the refrigerator but by opening God's Word and listening to his Spirit.

TURNING TOWARD GOD   Spiritual hunger has been described as a sense of yearning. When I look inside, there is a longing to be with God that pulls at my heart. I find I need to set aside time to be with God in worship, study and prayer.

How would you describe your sense of spiritual hunger?

How do you nourish yourself spiritually?

How is your inner attitude and outward behaviour affected by spiritual nourishment (or by the lack of it).

The Discipline of Obedience

God has called us to follow him. Sometimes we deliberately turn away from what we know he wants for us. At other times we wander from him on a gently meandering path. Whether we consciously turn away or just meander, both are acts of sin that take us out of the sense of God's presence. In contrast, obedience brings us close to God again. This Bible study and the application questions will help you to discover where you need to turn back toward God.

 **RECEIVING GOD'S WORD**   1. Read Isaiah 55. God extends an invitation in verses 1-2. Who is it to and what is offered?

2. Usually when we make a change or move through times of transition we are looking for ways to satisfy deep inner longings. Reflect on the challenge of verse 2. What do you think will bring you satisfaction and inner nourishment?

3. The substance of the "richest of fare" that God offers to feed our souls in verse 2 is a share in his covenant with King David. What did God promise to do for David and share with us (vv. 3-5)?

4. As the Son of David, Jesus Christ is the one for whom this covenant is ultimately fulfilled. How does the anticipation of sharing in Christ's splendour affect the way you are looking at your current circumstances?

5. Instead of an invitation to come to God, we are encouraged to pursue him. From verses 6-7, explain what it means to seek the Lord.

6. Even in the most godly people there is both a pursuit of the Lord and an avoidance of him. In what ways are you experiencing this attraction-avoidance dynamic in the current changes in your life?

7. In verses 8-9 God begins to contrast himself with the human race. What differences can you discern from this passage?

Why are the differences good news for us?

8. Look at verses 12-13. We have been invited by God to come to him and are encouraged to seek him. The passage now promises that we will be "going out." Describe what the "going out" is like.

9. These verses anticipate a time when the curse will be removed and creation will cease to grow thorns. Instead there will be a creation-wide celebration of God. How can such a perspective give you strength to continue following God in the midst of your current struggles and responsibilities?

God has all that we need to face the challenges of life. Ask him to give you a hunger for the rich fare he is waiting to give those who respond to his invitation.

NOW OR LATER   Fasting is a spiritual discipline that Christians have used through the centuries to be reminded that we don't live by bread alone. If your health allows it, why not try fasting for twenty-four hours? (That means skipping lunch, dinner and bedtime snacks.) Every time you feel a hunger pang, let it be a reminder that you are more hungry for spiritual food than you are for physical food. You might want to keep a running journal of your reflections and insights as you go through the day.

6

GOD'S UNCHANGING PROMISE

·····················
Practising the Discipline
of Prayer

When we find ourselves down the road a long way from where we started, even when we know God has called us, there come times of anxiety. We have questions about ourselves, and we have questions about God. For ourselves we have questions like, Is this what I really wanted? Am I really up to this challenge? And then we have questions for God like, Is he really with me? Will he keep his promises to me?

These sorts of questions can be debilitating. We become hung up in a loop of self-generating anxiety that continually feeds on itself. On the other hand, these questions can be focusing, clarifying and empowering.

What's the difference? Faith. As Abram followed God down the road he had a few questions for God. God is not at all put off by this. As a matter of fact, God responds with resounding affirmation to Abram's faithful questions.

The Discipline of Prayer

Prayer draws us close to God. It is an opportunity to give him our concerns and to listen for his voice. In prayer we may not always feel that we have connected with God, but as we remain faithful to seeking him, we will experience the riches of companionship with him. And our desire for and understanding of prayer grows as we study Scripture.

 **TURNING TOWARD GOD**   ✤God loves to answer our questions and respond to our needs. What questions do you have for God about the current challenges that you face? Make a list.

✤After you have made your list of concerns, consider prayerfully how the gift of God's continual presence with you might address some of the underlying concerns implicit in the challenges you face.

RECEIVING GOD'S WORD   1. Read Genesis 15:1-8. Abram is still in the beginning stages of his walk with God, perhaps within a year or two of moving from his previous home in Haran. What concerns might God be addressing as he encourages Abram not to be afraid?

2. God spoke to Abram in a vision, but he has many ways of addressing our concerns. What experiences, insights and encouragements have you received recently which, on reflection, might be from God?

3. God's assurances don't always immediately settle our anxieties

or resolve our concerns. What questions does Abram have for God in verses 2-8?

4. How do Abram's questions relate to the initial promises God made to Abram in Genesis 12:2-3?

5. The vision in which the word of the Lord comes to Abram could be described as a conversation that moves to deeper levels of understanding. What understanding do Abram and God come to in verses 4-6?

6. What experiences of prayer have you had that could be characterized as a conversation that moved you to a deeper level of understanding with God?

7. What is there about Abram's faith and God's response (v. 6) that can be a inspiration for and a model to you at this time in your life?

8. Read Genesis 15:9-21. In verse 8 we see that Abram feels a need for further assurance that he will inherit the land as God has promised. What assurance does God give him?

9. The cutting of the animals and walking between them is called "cutting a covenant." In Abram's time and culture it was the equivalent of signing a irrevocable contract. What does it say about God that he is willing to enter into a covenant (a binding contract) with Abram?

10. The death of Christ on the cross was God's binding contract for all people, in all times and all places. How can the knowledge of this covenant provide assurance for you now?

11. Before God confirms the covenant, he tells Abram what is in store for his descendants (vv. 12-14). What problems will they face?

12. The working out of God's promises or the assurance of his blessings does not mean that our lives or the circumstances of those we love will be trouble free. How will such perspective affect your prayers and expectations for the future?

As Abram pursued God for the assurance of his anxieties, spend some time focused in prayer, asking God to assure you of his presence, provision and protection.

NOW OR LATER   Several years ago I did a study of prayer from the Old Testament through to the New Testament. When I finished working my way through the pages and pages of material, I arrived at an insight that surprised me: Prayer is asking God to do what he has promised to do. Or in biblical terms, asking God to fulfill the terms of the covenant.

On reflection I realized I should have seen this all along. After all, prayer doesn't inform God of anything he does not already know. Nor is prayer persuading God to help us. He already wants to do that. Like any parent, God loves to provide for us. But like any good parent, God wants us to ask.

I began to see that the real difficulty at the heart of prayer is, Do I know what God has promised, and am I willing to ask for it? Abram knew what God promised and was able to ask God to keep his end of the bargain.

What has God promised you as a believer in Jesus Christ which applies to your current needs and circumstances? For the next week make a list of your prayers and keep it with you. In an attitude of faith, ask God to keep his covenant promises to you.

Guidelines for Leaders

My grace is sufficient for you. (2 Corinthians 12:9)

If leading a small group is something new for you, don't worry. These sessions are designed to be led easily. As a matter of fact, the flow of questions in the Bible study portions through the passage, from observation to interpretation to application, is so natural that you may feel the studies lead themselves.

You don't need to be an expert on the Bible or a trained teacher to lead a small group discussion. The idea behind these sessions is that the leader guides group members to discover for themselves what the Bible has to say and to listen for God's guidance. This method of learning will allow group members to remember much more of what is said than a lecture would.

This study guide is flexible. You can use it with a variety of groups—student, professional, neighbourhood or church groups. Each study takes forty-five to sixty minutes in a group setting.

There are some important facts to know about group dynamics and encouraging discussion. The suggestions listed below should enable you to fulfill your role as leader effectively and enjoyably.

Preparing for the Study

1. Ask God to help you understand and apply the passage in your own life. Unless this happens, you will not be prepared to lead others. Pray too for the various members of the group. Ask God to open your hearts to the message of his Word and motivate you to action.

2. Read the introduction to the entire guide to get an overview of the issues which will be explored.

3. As you begin each study, read and reread the assigned Bible passage to familiarize yourself with it.

4. This study guide is based on the New International Version of the Bible. It will help you and the group if you use this translation as the basis for your study and discussion.

5. Carefully work through each question in the study. Spend time in meditation and reflection as you consider how to respond.

6. Write your thoughts and responses in the space provided in the study guide. This will help you to express your understanding of the passage clearly.

7. It might help to have a Bible dictionary handy. Use it to look up any unfamiliar words, names or places. (For additional help on how to study a passage, see chapter five of *Leading Bible Discussions,* InterVarsity Press.)

8. Consider how you need to apply the Scripture to your life. Remember that the group will follow your lead in responding to the studies. They will not go any deeper than you do.

Leading the Study

1. Begin the study on time. Open with prayer, asking God to help the group understand and apply the passage.

2. Be sure that everyone in your group has a study guide. There are some questions and activities they will need to work through on their own, either beforehand or during the study session.

3. The flow of each study varies a bit. Many of the studies have time for silent reflection as well as for group discussion. Think through how you will lead the group through the times of silence, and read through the notes for guidance. It can be very powerful to have times of silence in the midst of a group session. Session four in particular focuses on silence and calls for an extended time apart. Then you can come together and share your experiences.

4. At the beginning of your first time together, explain that these studies are meant to be discussions, not lectures. Encourage the members of the group to participate. However, do not put pressure on those who may be hesitant to speak during the first few sessions. You may want to suggest the following guidelines to your group.

☐ Stick to the topic being discussed.

☐ Your responses should be based on the verses that are the focus of the discussion and not on outside authorities such as commentaries or speakers.

☐ These studies focus on a particular passage of Scripture. Only rarely should you refer to other portions of the Bible. This allows for everyone to participate on equal ground and for in-depth study.

☐ Anything said in the group is considered confidential and will not be discussed outside the group unless specific permission is given to do so.

☐ Provide time for each person present to talk if he or she feels comfortable doing so.

☐ Listen attentively to each other and learn from one another.

☐ Pray for each other.

5. Have a group member read the introduction at the beginning of the discussion.

6. Every session begins with the "Turning Toward God" section. The questions or activities are meant to be used before the passage is read. These questions introduce the theme of the study and encourage group members to begin to open up. Encourage as many members as possible to participate, and be ready to get the discussion going with your own response.

7. Either prior to or right after "Turning Toward God" you will see a definition of the specific discipline the session focuses on. Have someone read that explanation.

8. Have one or more group member(s) read aloud the passage to be studied.

9. As you ask the questions under "Receiving God's Word," keep in mind that they are designed to be used just as they are written. You may simply read them aloud, or you may prefer to express them in your own words.

There may be times when it is appropriate to deviate from the study guide. For example, a question may have already been answered. If so, move on to the next. Alternatively, someone may raise an important question not covered in the guide. Take time to discuss it, but try to keep the group from going off at a tangent.

10. Avoid answering your own questions. If necessary, repeat or rephrase them until they are clearly understood, or point out something you have read in the leader's notes to clarify the context or meaning. An eager group quickly becomes passive and silent if they think the leader will do most of the talking.

11. Don't be afraid of silence in response to the discussion questions. People may need time to think about the question before formulating their answers.

12. Don't be content with just one answer. Ask, "What do the rest of you think?" or "Anything else?" until several people have given answers to the question.

13. Acknowledge all contributions. Try to be affirming whenever possible. Never reject an answer. If it is clearly off-base, ask, "Which verse led you to that conclusion?" or again, "What do the rest of you think?"

14. Don't expect every answer to be addressed to you, even though this will probably happen at first. As group members become more at ease, they will begin to truly interact with each other. This is one sign of healthy discussion.

15. Don't be afraid of controversy. It can be very stimulating. If you don't resolve an issue completely, don't be frustrated. Move on and keep it in mind for later. A subsequent study may solve the problem.

16. Periodically summarize what the group has said about the passage. This helps to draw together the various ideas mentioned and gives continuity to the study. But don't preach.

17. At the end of the Bible discussion you may want to allow group members a time of quiet to work on an idea under "Now or Later." Then discuss what you experienced. Alternatively, you may want to encourage group members to work on these ideas between meetings. Give an opportunity during the session to allow people to talk about what they are learning.

18. Conclude your time together with conversational prayer,

adapting the prayer suggestion at the end of the study to your group. Ask for God's help in following through on the commitments you have made.

19. End on time.

Many more suggestions and helps are found in *Small Group Leader's Handbook* and *The Big Book on Small Groups* (both from InterVarsity Press), or *The Small-Group Leader* and *Small Group Starter Kit* (both from Scripture Union). Reading through one of these books would be worth your time.

Study Notes

Study 1. Called to Change. Genesis 12:1-9.
Purpose: To discern how God calls us away from all our attachments in order to be attached to him.

Turning Toward God. There are a number of questions here. If you are leading a group, use these questions to spend time getting people into the theme of the guide. Allow ten to fifteen minutes. It's okay if you don't get through all of the questions.

Question 1. The call of Abram was to receive a blessing in the land. Abram had to leave his homeland to take possession of it.

Question 3. Abram only had two sons in his lifetime, hardly a great nation. He never received ownership of the land during his lifetime, neither was his name great nor were all the peoples of the world blessed through him. These blessings came to him after his death, through his children. Ultimately, they came to him through Jesus Christ, a child born to his family some 2,000 years later. During Abram's lifetime, God did bless those who blessed Abram and cursed those who cursed him.

Question 4. Spiritual desires lie beyond all our dreams and wants. For instance, explore how a desire for a new house may be a desire to have a place of warmth and safety. Or how the desire for a new job may be to use our gifts and abilities to benefit others. Taken to the deepest levels all our hearts desires can be satisfied only by the love of God and grace of Jesus Christ. To draw the group out, you might also ask: How have your desires been met by faith in Jesus Christ? What desires are yet to be fulfilled?

Question 5. Abram traveled with his entire household, including his extended family. Explore how God's call to us has an impact far beyond our own personal experience.

Question 6. Recalling family vacations and moving from one place to another should provide plenty of material for a rousing discussion.

Question 7. It is a temptation to assume that God's direction and leading will bring smooth sailing and pleasant experiences. In verse 10, for instance, Abram experiences a famine in the land. **Questions 9-10.** Worship and prayer is the proper response to God's gracious guidance and blessing. Explore the times and places in which you are inspired to worship.

Study 2. Giving Our Fears to God. Exodus 14:5-31.

Purpose: To discover how we can trust God when change is threatening and dangerous.

Question 1. The Israelites had good reason to fear Pharaoh, who enslaved them and killed their children. Leaving Egypt, they were essentially a collection of slaves with no experience in battle or weapons to defend themselves.

Question 2. This question goes pretty deep. You may want to allow a time of silent reflection before you discuss it in a group. As you ask it, please be conscious that some members of your group may not feel comfortable answering it. For others, this question may provide opportunity to discover past fears that are still having an impact on their thoughts, attitudes, actions and relationships. Have one or more pray for the group as they confess these fears silently or aloud.

Question 3. Moses' answer to the people is quite remarkable. He is standing between a couple of million terrified slaves and an army. Yet in that pressurized situation, Moses projects confidence and assures Israel. However, the Lord's response to him in verse 15, "Why are you crying out to me?" implies that Moses did experience anxiety. Like a good leader, he took his fears to God rather than projecting them on his people.

Question 4. Remembering what God has done is the foundation for our present exercise of faith. The burning bush, the plagues, the Passover, were all demonstrations of God's presence with Moses. For Christians, the foundation of our trust in the Lord comes from his work in Scripture and from our past experience of providential guidance and answered prayer.

Question 5. Encourage members of your group to share their past experiences of God's hand. Help them to explore ways in which the resurrection of Christ (the ultimate demonstration of God's power) can give them a sense of present confidence.

Question 6. Just as it is possible to leave in response to God's call and yet stay in the same place (as we saw in the previous study), so it is possible to stand still and move out at the same time. "Standing still" is a settled attitude of rest and quiet in the depth of our hearts that comes from a faith-filled confidence in God.

Question 7. Here we have an opportunity to explore the role of prayer and the work of God. God doesn't need our prayers, but has chosen to work through our prayers to achieve his purposes. God chooses to make us important and so we are.

Question 8. God does not need us to achieve his purposes. However, he has chosen to work through our actions for his glory and our good. Explore ways that members of your group feel called to prayer and whether they feel their prayers are important.

Questions 12-13. Our response to God should include a deep respect that stirs us emotionally. Fear of the Lord comes from knowing deeply how powerful he is. This greatness produces confidence, courage and strength. Fear generated by circumstances comes from fear of danger and evil intent toward us. It takes away our confidence, courage and strength.

Study 3. Finding My New Place: 1 Corinthians 12:12-31.

Purpose: To discover how, especially in times of change, Christian community provides a place where we can belong.

Turning Toward God. If you are leading a study, you might ask people to discuss these questions in pairs for about five minutes.

Question 1. Spiritual unity is emphasized by Paul's repetition of the word *one*. However, it should be kept in mind that unity does not mean uniformity. Being one in Christ does not do away with different social status or racial identity.

Question 2. This application creates opportunity for positive appreciation of involvement in the church. This is important because the next question looks at problems in the church.

Question 3. This question may bring up some deep pains and frustrations about the church. That's okay. Airing frustrations now will set up later questions which explore a means of overcoming those frustrations.

Someone has commented that Sunday morning at 11:00 is the most segregated hour in the nation. It is also the time when people of the same social status and income are gathered. Help your group explore why we tend to exclude those who are not like us, even in the church.

Question 4. This can be a fun but also threatening question because it invites self-exposure. Seek to create a warm and affirming environment that encourages open discussion.

Question 6. When we move from one place to another, there is a temptation to think that we can assume the same role and function within the new church. Often, however, someone else already has that role. Tension and conflict can result. We need to understand that our gifts and callings can change. God frequently gives us spiritual gifts based on the needs of the church.

Question 8. These verses deal with the importance of differences and interdependence within the Christian community. Christians have often confused unity with uniformity. Paul's teaching in this passage is an important corrective to such misunderstanding.

Steve Taylor wrote a song in the 1980s entitled "I want to Be a Clone." The refrain went, "If you are going to be one of his, you have to act like one of us."

Question 9. Not all the spiritual gifts are mentioned in these verses. After exploring how the gifts mentioned here contribute to building a strong Christian community, feel free to consider how other gifts contribute as well. The apostle Paul's point in this study is that we need each other. This question encourages members of your group to consider how they are not self-sufficient and independent of the care and support of others.

Question 11. You can discuss these questions as a whole group or with partners. Set an affirming tone. Seek to bring out specific incidents that illustrate and affirm the existence and use of spiritual gifts in each of the members of your group.

Question 12. This is an important question for this entire theme of meeting God in times of change. During times of transition people often feel better when they have helped someone else.

Study 4. Discerning God's Direction. Psalm 32:6-11.

Purpose: To explore how we can discern God's guidance and direction for our lives in the midst of our doubts.

General Note. If you are leading a group, consider meeting in a setting that will allow you to separate for quiet reflection—for example, at a church or in a quiet park. Open with prayer and perhaps some worshipful singing. Then allow forty-five minutes to an hour to work through the material in "Turning Toward God" and "Receiving from God." Encourage people to find a place of privacy. Encourage them to write in response to the questions and to sit in silence, listening and reflecting on God. Then come together to talk about what you experienced and how God spoke through the passage.

Question 2. This psalm portrays God as a safe place, a "hiding place" where we can go for safety and direction. It should be noted that God is a safe place for those who come to him with their sin. Our natural response is to run *from* him; the spiritual response is to run *to* him. It is in confession and fellowship that we can settle down, get quiet and hear the direction of the Lord.

Concerning leading and guiding, God promises to "instruct us and teach us in the way that we should go" (v. 8). Someone has commented that God is always speaking, but we aren't always listening. If we are to listen, then we must trust him and settle down within ourselves so that we can hear. This meditative study and the accompanying exercises will help you do this.

Study 5. Resources for the Journey. Isaiah 55.

Purpose: To discover how God provides the resources and strength we need to face the challenges of change and transition.

Question 1. The context of Isaiah 55 is Israel's exile. Isaiah was looking ahead to the time when God's people would be taken captive to Babylon. After a period of judgement God promises to bring them back and restore their land. As God brings them back, he promises to feed those who are hungry.

Question 3. The Davidic covenant can be found in 2 Samuel 7:5-16. In many ways it is similar to the Abrahamic covenant in Genesis 12. God promises to make David's name great, to be with him wherever he goes, to provide a safe land. David's royal line will be established and one of David's sons will the final king. In addition, God promises to adopt that son as his own. The Davidic covenant is fulfilled in Jesus Christ.

Question 4. This question is a challenge for many Christians raised in the here-and-now emphasis of modern secular culture. It is a discipline for us to look beyond our current circumstances to both the blessings of heaven and the final and complete consummation of the kingdom of God on earth. That hope, if embraced in faith, keeps us from being carried away by immediate pleasures or painful burdens.

Question 5. If we want to be with God, we must live the way he wants us to—in righteousness—and we must turn to him for for-giveness when we fail to live up to his Word.

Question 6. We can judge our pursuit of the Lord by our hunger for Scripture, our desire for prayer and our avoidance of sin. In addition, when we are pursuing God there is a deep, almost spontaneous sense of gratitude that wells up within our hearts. When we are avoiding God, there is little interest in prayer or Scripture study and God is seldom on our minds. In such a state we are seldom thankful.

If you are leading a group, you may want to allow time for silent confession and prayer here.

Question 7. God is dependable and powerful in contrast to humans, who are weak and fickle. Because God is dependable and powerful, we can trust him completely.

Question 8. There is a harmony in creation in which we are invited to joyfully share. We can go anywhere with freedom and safety. The promised land becomes the entire world.

Study 6. God's Unchanging Promise. Genesis 15.

Purpose: To see how God gives us an assurance we can depend on in the uncertainties and challenges of life.

Turning Toward God. This exercise should be completed in private reflection. Give your group members about ten minutes to list their needs and to pray alone or with partners.

Question 1. Abram has not yet been given the land as his own possession, nor have he and Sara had any children. In the beginning stages of a walk with the Lord, a couple of years seems like a long time. It would be over twenty years before Isaac was born.

Question 2. God is speaking to us. The issue is, do we know how to listen? God speaks to us through Scripture, circumstances in our lives, advice from friends and family, and the desires of our hearts. Time spent in prayerful discernment helps us listen for the voice of God in all these areas and more.

Questions 3-4. Abram wants to know how he can be sure that God is actually going to give him the land and when he is going to have the children he was promised.

Question 5. God assures Abram that he will keep his promise to give him many children. Abram's response of faith to God's promise and the gift of righteousness becomes the foundation for the apostle Paul's teaching that salvation in Christ comes as a gift of righteousness to all who believe.

Question 6. This question requires a good deal of reflection. You may want to allow a time of silence for people to ponder. Journaling is also a great help in listening and discerning.

Question 7. Abram was able both to ask God for assurance when he was frustrated and to trust God when he was assured.

Question 8. God gives him a glimpse of the future and a covenant.

Question 9. That God, the Creator, would be willing to bind himself to a covenant is stunning. The Christian God is the covenant God. There is a branch of Christianity that embraces "Covenant theology" and sees the concept of covenant as one of the central organizing themes of Scripture. That God makes a covenant demonstrates his desire to provide assurance for us and a solid foundation for our faith.

Question 10. Jesus makes the new covenant during the Last Supper; see Luke 22:20. The promises of the kingdom of God and eternal life beyond death mean that nothing that happens to us is ultimately fatal. On the contrary, it implies, as Paul says in Romans 8:28, "that in all things God works for the good of those who love him, who have been called according to his purpose."

Questions 11-12. Our salvation on this side of heaven is a "suffering salvation." The entire book of 1 Peter is given over to exploring the surprise and challenge that suffering brings to Christians. Peter concludes with the following benediction: "And the God of all grace, who called you to his eternal glory in Christ, after you have suffered a little while, will himself restore you and make you strong, firm and steadfast. To him be the power for ever and ever. Amen" (5:10-11).